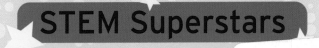

STEM Superstars

Tim Berners-Lee

by Mari Bolte

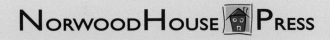

NORWOOD HOUSE PRESS

Cover: Tim Berners-Lee's work shaped how people use the internet.

Norwood House Press
For information regarding Norwood House Press, please visit our website at:
www.norwoodhousepress.com or call 866-565-2900.

Hardcover ISBN: 978-1-68450-661-3
Paperback ISBN: 978-1-68404-996-7
eBook ISBN: 978-1-68404-276-0

Library of Congress Cataloging-in-Publication Data
Library of Congress Cataloging-in-Publication Data has been filed and is available at catalog.loc.gov

372N—012024
Manufactured in the United States of America in North Mankato, Minnesota.

★ Table of Contents ★

Chapter 1

Early Life

Tim Berners-Lee was born on June 8, 1955. He is from London, England. His parents worked with computers. They had a daughter and two other sons.

⭐ **Berners-Lee grew up in southwest London.**

4

Many trains go through London. As a kid, Berners-Lee watched them go by his school.

Berners-Lee liked math and computers. He also really liked trains. Berners-Lee had a train set. He learned how it worked. He built new controllers for it.

Berners-Lee went to Oxford University in 1973. He studied **physics**. He made his own computer. It was built from old TVs.

In the 1970s, computers were large. They had many different parts.

Chapter 2

Weaving the Web

In the 1980s, computers did not do as much. People could send messages. But sharing **files** was hard. Computers did not speak the same language. Berners-Lee wanted to fix that.

Berners-Lee's work with math and electronics helped him find ways to make computers better.

11

Berners-Lee wrote three **programs**. URLs were like information maps. HTTP turned those maps into a live link. HTML put URLs into messages. All computers could use the programs.

Berners-Lee did his most important work on this computer in Switzerland.

Berners-Lee wants the Web to be a tool for communicating.

Did You Know?
Building the Web took three years.

Berners-Lee wrote more **software**. It let people look at and change files. He called it the World Wide Web, or Web. Now, people could share freely.

Chapter 3

An Open World

People offered Berners-Lee money. They wanted to own his invention. He said no. He wanted the Web to be free and open to anyone.

Berners-Lee shared the blueprints for the Web. Anyone with a computer and internet access could build from it.

Queen Elizabeth II knighted Berners-Lee in 2004.

Berners-Lee started a group in 1994. It is the World Wide Web **Consortium**. He is the director. He works to make the internet safe and fair.

Berners-Lee could have sold the Web. He could have been a billionaire. Instead, he gave it to the people. Now, anyone can explore the Web.

Berners-Lee now works at the Massachusetts Institute of Technology.

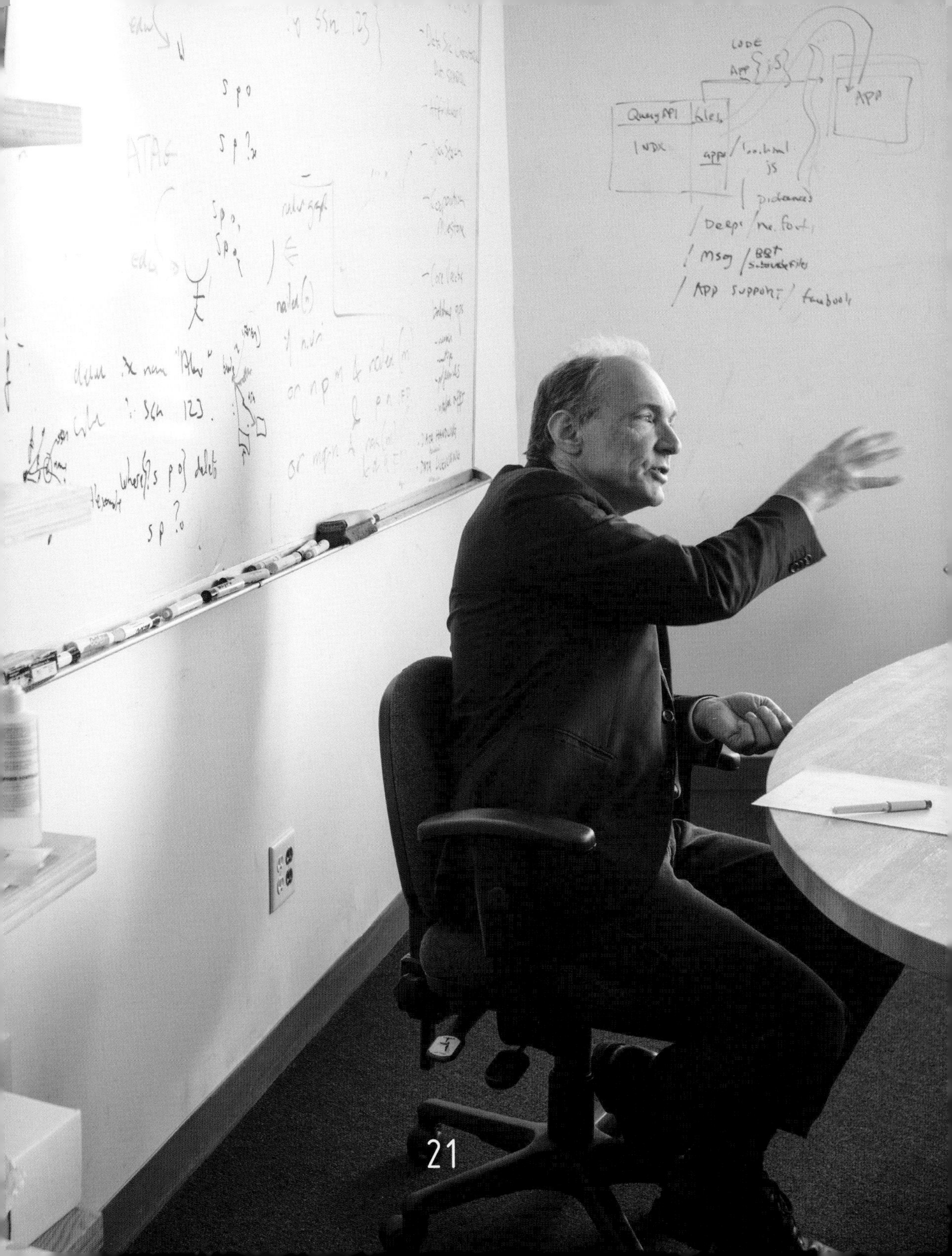

★ Career Connections ★

1 Berners-Lee was interested in trains and electronics as a child. He turned that interest into a career. Make a list of the things you like. With an adult's help, go online. Find three jobs that have to do with your interests.

2 The Web changed the way people communicate. Most people use cell phones, text messages, and email every day. Write a story about what life would be like without these tools.

3 Coders write programs called code. Code tells computers what to do. Coders might design an app. They might test a program to make sure it works well. They might even work on the next big video game! Imagine you are a computer coder. What kind of work would you do?

4 Every piece of technology was invented by someone! Pick one tool that you use often. It could be from your home or school. With an adult's help, go online. Research who invented or improved that tech.

★ Glossary ★

consortium (kahn-SOR-shum): A group of people, companies, organizations, or governments that work together for a common goal.

files (FY-uhls): Places to record and store info on a computer.

internet (IN-ter-net): A global network of computers all connected to each other.

knighted (NAI-tuhd): Given the rank of knight, an honor for helping the United Kingdom.

physics (FIH-ziks): A branch of science that deals with matter and energy.

programs (PRO-grams): Instructions for a computer to do a task automatically.

software (SAHFT-wehr): Programs and other information used by a computer.

★ For More Information ★

Books

Castro, Rachel. *Shigeru Miyamoto*. Chicago, IL: Norwood House Press, 2020. Read about a superstar video game developer.

Smibert, Angie. *Computers from Then to Now*. Mankato, MN: Amicus, 2020. Learn more about the history of computer technology.

Websites

Scratch
(https://scratch.mit.edu/) Learn to create computer code with MIT's free Scratch program.

Tim Berners-Lee
(https://kids.britannica.com/kids/article/Tim-Berners-Lee/626687) Learn more about the inventor of the World Wide Web.

★ Index ★

★ About the Author ★

Mari Bolte loves history and sharing its lessons with others. She has written and edited books on many different subjects. She lives in Minnesota surrounded by animals and the woods.